For Charl

With all my love,
We are allies in grief
and allies in our
love for Jesus.
        love,
        Adolfo

The Teachings of Jesus

Adolfo Quezada

The Teachings of Jesus
Interpreted for Everyday Living

Adolfo Quezada

Also by Adolfo Quezada

Compassionate Presence
Radical Love
Sabbath Moments
Transcending Illness Through the Power of Belief
Loving Yourself for God's Sake
Wholeness: The Legacy of Jesus
Walking with God
Goodbye My Son, Hello
Rising from the Ashes
A Desert Place
Heart Peace
Through the Darkness

To my wife Judy who is my love, my inspiration, and my constant personal and professional support.

How to Use this Book

The Teachings of Jesus: Interpreted for Everyday Living is intended to be read slowly and in small measures. It can be used as a companion in contemplation, prayer, and in the practice of *lectio divina* (contemplative reading). It is invaluable as a spiritual guide, and can serve as a resource for pastoral ministry, Bible studies, and spiritual dialogue groups.

Table of Contents

Preface   15

Chapter One
About My Father's Business   17

    How Jesus Taught   19

    What Jesus Taught   21
        Beyond Survival   21
        Responsible Faith   21
        Only God Alone   22
        Now is the Time   22
        Commitment   22
        The Narrow Gate   23
        Your Soul Belongs to God   23
        Living for God   24

Chapter Two
Listen to another Parable   25

    The Realm of Heaven   27
        The Foolish Bridesmaids   27
        The Growing Seed   28
        The Wedding Feast   28
        The Laborers in the Vineyard   30
        The Treasure   31
        The Unmerciful Servant   31
        The Weeds Among the Wheat   32
        The Leaven   33
        The Mustard Seed   33
        The Net   33
        The Pearl   34

Other Parables of Jesus — 35
    The Prodigal Son — 35
    The Prodigal Son (continued) — 36
    The Lost Sheep — 37
    The Wedding Guest — 38
    The Faithful Servant — 38
    The Grateful King — 39
    The Fig Tree — 40
    The Shrewd Manager — 40
    The Rich Fool — 42
    A House Divided — 42
    Overcoming Evil — 43
    The Friend at Midnight — 43
    The Two Debtors — 43
    Lazarus — 44
    The Good Samaritan — 45
    The Wise and Foolish Builders — 46
    The Unclean Spirit — 47
    The Lost Coin — 47
    The Sower — 48
    The Wicked Tenants — 48
    The Unjust Judge — 50
    The Pharisee and Tax Collector — 50
    The Two Sons — 51
    The Talents — 52

Chapter Three
Truly I Tell You

55

Beatitudes — 57
    Poverty — 57
    Grief — 57
    Humility — 57
    Yearning for God — 58
    Forgiveness — 58
    Single-Heartedness — 58
    Peace — 59
    Courage — 59

Love above All   61
    You Shall Love   61
    Love of Enemies   61
    Treatment of Others   62
    Judgment   62
    Words   63
    Reconciled Heart   63
    Forgiveness   64
    Little Ones   64

Sharing with Others   65
    Beyond the Commandments   65
    Possessions   65
    Giving and Receiving   66
    Riches   66
    Secret Charity   67
    Give What You Have   67

Precious Human Beings   69
    Goodness   69
    Passion for Life   69
    Light   70
    Let the Children Come   70

Justice   71
    Oaths   71
    Love and Goodness is the Law   71
    Something Greater   72
    Vengeance   72

Wholeness   75
    Enlightenment   75
    The Cloak   75
    The Wineskins   76
    Moral Cancer   76
    Faith   76
    Fear of Death   77
    Anxiety   77
    Merciful Healing   78

Treasure of the Heart   78
Public Piety   79
Rest for Your Soul   79
Private Fasting   79
Become Childlike   80

Beware   81
Trust but Verify   81
Beware of Religious Hierarchy   81
Blind Guides   82
Fruits of Consciousness   82
Interpreting Signs   82

Chapter Four
Pray Always   85

Pray Then in This Way   87
In Secret   87
With Sincerity   87
With Faith   88
It Will Be Done   88
Ask, Search, Knock   88
Keep Awake   89

Jesus Prays   91
The Lord's Prayer   91
Revelation   91
Remove This Cup   92
Forgive Them   92
Forsaken   92
Into Your Hands   93

Chapter Five
Follow Me 95

Cost of Discipleship   97
    Follow Me   97
    Estimating the Cost   97
    Proclaiming the Good News   98
    Wise and Innocent   98
    Reveal the Truth   99
    Welcome   99
    Acknowledge   100
    Arrive in Peace, Leave in Peace   100
    Serve Without Recompense   100
    Truth   101
    Go Where You Are Needed   101
    The Greatest Among You   101
    A Desert Place   102
    Endurance   102
    Family against Family   103
    Trust the Spirit   103
    Before the Loss   103
    War   104
    Stay Awake   104
    Dying to Self   104
    The Way of the Cross   105

Preface

Before organized Christianity and church doctrine existed, there were the pure and powerful words of Jesus. His sapient teachings have impacted humanity through the millennia, and the essence of what he taught is as relevant to us today as it was to his contemporaries.

Jesus was not directing his words to 21st century men and women. His teachings were meant to be pertinent and relevant to those of his time, geographic location, and historical circumstances. Yet his teachings transcend history and geography; they reach beyond time, culture and religion. Jesus taught universal truths that appeal to men and women of all religions as well as to the nonreligious.

In twenty five years of practicing counseling and psychotherapy I learned that the men and women who sought spiritual help from me were not interested in religious doctrine or prescribed dogma. Rather, they wanted first of all to be understood as human beings. Their spiritual quest was simply to learn from life and grow to their full potential. They were drawn to spiritual teachings, not as much by who taught them as by how applicable they were in their daily life. It was with this realization in mind that I decided to write *The Teachings of Jesus: Interpreted for Everyday Living*.

Many of Jesus' teachings are familiar to us. Some we have heard frequently in the course of our life. Yet the familiar is often taken for granted and not considered in depth. Poetic phrases may be appreciated for their symmetry yet not have an impact on our daily living. My intent in writing this book was to encourage a fresh look at the words of Jesus and to promote a more profound consideration of their significance for all human beings, regardless of their religious affiliation or spiritual tradition.

The Teachings of Jesus: Interpreted for Everyday Living does not purport to be an account of the life of Jesus, and it is not an exhaustive record of his sayings. Instead, it focuses specifically on what Jesus taught to the crowds who followed him, to the religious and civic authorities that persecuted him, and to his disciples who followed him then, and those who follow him now.

I concentrated on the teachings of Jesus as recorded in the three Synoptic Gospels: Matthew, Mark, and Luke. The Synoptic Gospels, which were written within thirty or forty years of Jesus' death, are referred to as "synoptic" because they take a common view regarding the life and teachings of Jesus. Using *lectio divina* (contemplative reading), I pondered extensively each phrase that Jesus uttered. Then, using contemporary language that retained the essence of his meaning, I interpreted his words as they spoke to me.

Chapter One, *About My Father's Business,* is about Jesus' teaching ministry. Chapter Two, *Listen to another Parable,* includes his compelling short stories which stimulated the imagination of his followers and awakened them to the realm of heaven. Chapter Three, *Truly I Tell You,* consists of Jesus' short sayings of common truth. Chapter Four, *Pray Always,* includes the prayers of Jesus and what he taught regarding prayer. Chapter Five, *Follow Me,* considers the cost of discipleship.

Though the voice of Jesus was vehement and his message was clear, his recorded words are relatively few. As far as we know, nothing Jesus said was written down during his lifetime. Some of what he taught was passed on through the generations by word-of-mouth, but the recorded words probably include only a fraction of all that Jesus taught. We can only imagine how much more Jesus said that was not recorded. Yet, these are the words we have before us. I invite you to read and ponder them, and allow them to speak to your mind, your heart, and your spirit.

My hope is that through this book of Jesus' teachings, and the interpretations I offer, you may discover that his words have a deeper dimension than the purely literal, and when understood, can lead you to deeper spiritual growth.

Adolfo Quezada
Tucson, Arizona
April 8, 2014

Chapter One
About My Father's Business

As a young boy Jesus was found by his parents asking questions of the teachers in the temple. He said to his parents, "Did you not know I must be about my Father's business" (Lk 2:49)? As an adult, Jesus respected the authority of the religious leaders of his time, yet he departed radically from what they taught. Instead, he taught according to the promptings of God. In fact, the God Jesus knew most intimately was the one he encountered in life. God was the center of his life; everything else flowed from that.

How Jesus Taught

Essentially, Jesus was a teacher of living fully and loving wholeheartedly. He had a brilliant mind, yet he spoke from his heart; he appealed to the people's reason and common sense, yet he spoke to their hearts. He answered questions, told stories, and drew parallels between natural phenomena and life experiences. He did not lecture, but instead commented on what he saw and heard in the moment before him.

Jesus was not a teacher in the conventional sense. He didn't just present information for his disciples to absorb. Rather, he taught in such a way that his followers were awakened to possibilities they had never before considered, and were exposed to an intimacy with God they had never before dared.

Jesus taught in the countryside, on the seashore, on the mountainside, and on the dusty roads. He taught simple peasants and fishermen from the little towns of Galilee. Few of Jesus' contemporaries were literate, but they listened to his teachings and passed on to others what they heard. He had many followers, but eventually he invited only twelve men into his intimate circle to learn from him and carry on his teaching ministry.

Jesus expressed himself using prose and metaphor. He used parables, paradoxes, and Galilean folklore, and he personalized his words to make them relevant to his followers. He took life situations and used them to make his point. He spoke of beauty, hope, and possibility. He was witty and sometimes sarcastic. He did not hesitate to use fantasy to teach about reality. His extreme language captured the attention of his followers, his exaggerations shocked them, and his vivid descriptions sparked their imagination.

Whether it was a lily or a sparrow, a cloud or the wind, Jesus revered God's handiwork. "Behold!" was a favorite word of his. He beheld the world through the eyes of a child: freshly, innocently, and purely. He looked upon a bird in awe and wonderment. A grain of wheat for him was a miracle waiting to happen. Everything and everyone was precious and needed to be experienced with a grateful heart. From the smallest seed to the largest mountain, Jesus marveled.

Jesus embraced his humanity to the fullest, including the joy and suffering that are intrinsic to life. He retreated often from the rigors of living as an itinerant teacher. He would climb a mountain to meditate or venture into the wilderness to be alone, but always he remained connected to the people whom he was committed to serve.

Jesus looked upon God as his "Father in heaven." Among the first recorded words of Jesus were, "Did you not know that I must be about my Father's business" (Lk 2:49)? And among the last recorded words of his life were, "Father, into your hands I commend my spirit" (Lk 23:46). His perception of God as "Father" was not anthropomorphic; that is, he did not look upon God as one would look upon one's earthly father. Rather, the fatherhood of God had more to do with Jesus' intimate relationship with God whom he believed to be his source and destiny.

The God in whom Jesus believed was a loving, tender, encouraging father who offered the intimacy of oneness. In fact, Jesus called him by the more endearing and personal name of "Abba," which meant papa or daddy. Jesus believed that all human beings were sons and daughters of God, and that this designation brought with it great responsibility. That responsibility, according to Jesus, was not to be obedient to religious laws, but to be fully human and to serve humankind in the name of God.

The teachings of Jesus were unific, that is, they were based on the belief that, ultimately, everyone is connected to everyone else. He taught about union amid diversity, community among the multitude, and inclusion of the excluded.

Jesus believed that his life was a response to God's calling. One of the ways Jesus chose to respond was to teach others how to live in and for God. At thirty years of age he began to teach. He taught with his words and he taught with his life. He walked the paths that led him to where the people were and, eventually, he was compelled by those who opposed him to walk the path to his crucifixion.

What Jesus Taught

Before beginning his teaching ministry, Jesus was drawn into the desert. Withdrawal into the wilderness of the desert or the remoteness of a mountain was important to him, for he knew that this was where he found his ground of being. In prayer and meditation, in solitude and silence, he was fully conscious of the divine essence within him.

The desert strips a man of the superfluous. From that dry and barren place, Jesus emerged with a sense of urgency. More than ever he believed that life was precious and must not be squandered even for a moment. He reentered the world, exhorting those whom he encountered to turn their lives around. He taught them that the present moment was the time to enter the realm of heaven.

Beyond Survival

One does not live by bread alone, but by every word that comes from the mouth of God.

Mt 1:9-11

Interpretation: Beyond the nourishment, for which your body hungers, is the expression of God for which your soul incessantly yearns. When you focus primarily on your physical needs instead of God, you overlook your greatest need of all: your communion with God in silent surrender and loving attention.

Responsible Faith

Again, it is written, "Do not put the Lord your God to the test."

Mt 4:7

Interpretation: Faith is prudent and respects the laws of nature. Denial of natural and logical consequences of your actions is not faith, but madness. It is not God's willingness to protect you that should be tested, but your willingness to live according to the ways of God.

For God Alone

Away with you, Satan! for it is written, "Worship the Lord your God, and serve only him."

Mt 4:10

Interpretation: The gods of your unconscious self tempt you toward malice, yet your heart belongs to your Beloved, who embraces your soul as well. Were it never written, it would still be true: your reverence is for God alone. Your love for God is the foundation of your life and the purpose of your being.

Now is the Time

The time is fulfilled, and the kingdom of God has come near; repent, and believe in the good news.

Mk 1:15

Interpretation: Right here, right now, God is within you and without you. Turn and begin anew; believe in your power to transform. What has come before can be forgiven. What you do with the moment before you is all that matters.

Commitment

No one can serve two masters; for a slave will either hate the one and love the other, or be devoted to the one and despise the other. You cannot serve God and wealth.

Mt 6:24

Interpretation: You face the same decision many times a day: whether to live in the service of temporal wealth or dedicate your service to that which lasts forever. Commit to one, for to choose both is to commit to neither. Let nothing compete with God for your love or impede the work you do on God's behalf.

The Narrow Gate

Enter through the narrow gate; for the gate is wide and the road is easy that leads to destruction, and there are many who take it. For the gate is narrow and the road is hard that leads to life, and there are few who find it.

Mt 7:13-14

Interpretation: The way of true and authentic living is difficult to find, and once found is hard to live. Few are those who discover it and fewer still those who traverse it to the end. You may start down wrongful paths or you may take the roads that lead you nowhere. It is only when you realize that you have gone astray, and then ask for guidance from within, that the threshold of true life opens before you; and the arduous journey toward wholeness begins.

Your Soul Belongs to God

Give to the emperor the things that are the emperor's and to God the things that are God's.

Mk 12:17

Interpretation: The powers of the world can exact from you all that you possess, but give only to God the essence of your being. Share from your holdings for the benefit of the whole and give to the community its due, but save your soul for God alone, it is where God abides. Cling to nothing that can be taken from you, including your life on earth. But remember, the core of your existence belongs to God.

Living for God

Not everyone who says to me, "Lord, Lord," will enter the kingdom of heaven, but only the one who does the will of my Father in heaven. On that day many will say to me, "Lord, Lord, did we not prophecy in your name, and cast out demons in your name, and do many deeds of power in your name?" Then I will declare to them, "I never knew you; go away from me, you evildoers."

Mt 7:21-23

Interpretation: The realm of heaven is not yours because you deserve it; and neither can you earn it. Rather, it comes to you when you seek God at the depth of your being through prayer and meditation, and live your days in congruence with the ways of God.

Chapter Two
Listen to another Parable

Jesus invited his followers to "Listen to another parable" (Mt 21:33). When he taught in parables his teachings were esoteric, veiled, and mysterious because he was counting on the perceptivity of the soul. A constant theme in his parables was what he referred to as the "kingdom of God" or "the kingdom of heaven." In this book it is referred to as "the realm of heaven." Jesus described the realm of heaven in myriad ways.

The Realm of Heaven

For Jesus, the realm of heaven was not a place or an earthly authority; rather, it was the dimension of life toward which our soul evolves. He taught that the nature of the realm of heaven was to grow and develop from the smallest to the largest, from the most vulnerable to the most invulnerable, and from the weakest to the most potent. He taught that the realm of heaven was not imperial, but personal, and was founded on the love between God and the human soul. The realm of heaven, according to Jesus, contained the eternal within the temporal and the whole within the part.

The Foolish Bridesmaids

Then the kingdom of heaven will be like this. Ten bridesmaids took their lamps and went to meet the bridegroom. Five of them were foolish, and five were wise. When the foolish took their lamps, they took no oil with them; but the wise took flasks of oil with their lamps. As the bridegroom was delayed, all of them became drowsy and slept. But at midnight there was a shout, "Look! Here is the bridegroom! Come out to meet him." Then all those bridesmaids got up and trimmed their lamps. The foolish said to the wise, "Give us some of your oil, for our lamps are going out." But the wise replied, "No! There will not be enough for you and for us; you had better go to the dealers and buy some for yourselves." And while they went to buy it, the bridegroom came, and those who were ready went with him into the wedding banquet; and the door was shut. Later the other bridesmaids came also, saying, "Lord, lord, open to us." But he replied, "Truly I tell you, I do not know you." Keep awake therefore, for you know neither the day nor the hour.

Mt 25:1-13

Interpretation: You must prepare for the unknown time when the divine breaks into your life. Some of you prepare daily through prayer and meditation for such occasions in which the heavenly and the earthly are joined within you. Some of you prepare only partially. You fulfill religious obligations and perform customary rituals, but fail to internalize the spirit. Consequently, you come to know about God, but you do not know God.

You are called to enter daily into a deep and personal relationship with God so that you can be ready to be received into the realm of heaven on a moment's notice. The brilliance of your enlightenment alone is not enough; there must also be depth of understanding and perseverance of faith, even through the darkness.

The Growing Seed

The kingdom of God is as if someone would scatter seed on the ground and would sleep and rise night and day, and the seed would sprout and grow, he does not know how. The earth produces of itself, first the stalk, then the head, then the full grain in the head. But when the grain is ripe, at once he goes in with his sickle, because the harvest has come.

Mk 4:26-29

Interpretation: God infuses new life into the womb of humanity where it mysteriously gestates for a time. The divine essence is hidden deep in the soil of the soul, but there comes a time for it to burst into the light in splendid fruition. There is a time to sow and a time to reap. There is a time for sacrifice and a time for dying into new life.

The Wedding Feast

The kingdom of heaven may be compared to a king who gave a wedding banquet for his son. He sent his slaves to call those who had been invited to the wedding banquet, but they would not come. Again he sent other slaves, saying, "Tell those who have been invited: 'Look, I have prepared my dinner, my oxen, and my fat calves have been slaughtered and everything is ready; come to the wedding banquet.'" But they made light of it and went away, one to his farm, another to his business, while the rest seized his slaves, mistreated them, and killed them. The king was enraged. He sent his troops, destroyed those murderers, and burned their city. Then he said to his slaves, "The wedding is ready, but those invited were not worthy. Go therefore into the main streets, and invite everyone you find to the wedding banquet." Those slaves went out into the streets and gathered all whom they found, both good and bad; so the wedding hall was filled with guests.

But when the king came to see the guests, he noticed a man there who was not wearing a wedding robe, and he said to him, "Friend, how did you get in here without a wedding robe?" And he was speechless. Then the king said to the attendants, "Bind him hand and foot, and throw him into the outer darkness, where there will be weeping and gnashing of teeth." For many are called, but few are chosen.

Mt 22:2-14

Interpretation: You are beckoned by God to celebrate the union of heaven and earth. You are asked by God to witness and participate in the nuptials of divinity and humanity. You are invited into the realm of heaven to drink the nectar of God and be nourished by the bread of life. But some of you are too busy to partake. You have placed your priority on less important matters. You are concerned with the accumulation and protection of wealth, you are preoccupied with worldly responsibilities, and you are distracted by mind-numbing entertainment. There are many reasons why you cannot or will not respond to God's persistent bidding. In fact, you silence the voices within you that summon you to the realm of heaven. The consequence of your refusal to enter the light of consciousness is that you are left outside in the darkness of unconsciousness. There is no greater grief than to be separated from God.

God persists in the gathering of souls. No one is excluded who is willing to come. The good, the bad, the rich, the poor, the religious, the nonreligious, all are invited. But once you accept the invitation and enter the realm of heaven, you must change in order to stay. You cannot remain the person you have been. You cannot wear the cloak of insincerity or be arrayed in the apparel of impropriety. You cannot be clad in sheep's clothing, yet remain a calculating, opportunistic, selfish wolf at heart. Such interloping is not allowed and soon you find yourself on the outside looking in. Those who sincerely accept God's invitation don the raiment of transformation. All are invited, but only the pure in heart may stay.

The Laborers in the Vineyard

For the kingdom of heaven is like a landowner who went out early in the morning to hire laborers for his vineyard. After agreeing with the laborers for the usual daily wage, he sent them into his vineyard. When he went out about nine o'clock, he saw others standing idle in the marketplace; and he said to them, "You also go into the vineyard, and I will pay you whatever is right." So they went. When he went out again about noon and about three o'clock, he did the same. And about five o'clock he went out and found others standing around; and he said to them, "Why are you standing here idle all day?" They said to him, "Because no one has hired us." He said to them, "You also go into the vineyard." When evening came, the owner of the vineyard said to his manager, "Call the laborers and give them their pay, beginning with the last and then going to the first." When those hired about five o'clock came, each of them received the usual daily wage. Now when the first came, they thought they would receive more; but each of them also received the usual daily wage. And when they received it, they grumbled against the landowner, saying, "These last worked only one hour, and you have made them equal to us who have borne the burden of the day and the scorching heat." But he replied to one of them, "Friend, I am doing you no wrong; did you not agree with me for the usual daily wage? Take what belongs to you and go; I choose to give to this last the same as I gave to you. Am I not allowed to do what I choose with what belongs to me? Or are you envious because I am generous?" So the last will be first, and the first will be last.

Mt 20:1-16

Interpretation: The realm of heaven is offered to everyone. Some come to it early in life, some come late. Some live exemplary lives, some do not. Each life is different. Each covenant is a matter between the individual soul and God and cannot be compared with others. The realm of heaven is not a reward or payment for a life well lived. You cannot demand it nor can you compete with others for it. You do not deserve it and you cannot earn it. The realm of heaven is a beatific state that is your inheritance as a son or daughter of God. The key to its gate is a humble, grateful, and open heart.

The Treasure

The kingdom of heaven is like treasure hidden in a field, which someone found and hid; then in his joy he goes and sells all that he has and buys that field.

Mt 13:44

Interpretation: The most precious treasure of all is the realm of heaven that lies hidden in your soul. When you find it you are joyous, yet you keep it hidden lest it be plundered by the forces of your unconscious self. In order to make the realm of heaven your own, you must give up all you possess for that which gains you this ultimate wealth.

The Unmerciful Servant

For this reason the kingdom of heaven may be compared to a king who wished to settle accounts with his slaves. When he began the reckoning, one who owed him ten thousand talents was brought to him; and, as he could not pay, his lord ordered him to be sold, together with his wife and children and all of his possessions, and payment to be made. So the slave fell on his knees before him, saying, "Have patience with me, and I will pay you everything." And out of pity for him, the lord of that slave released him and forgave him the debt. But that same slave, as he went out, came upon one of his fellow slaves who owed him a hundred denarri; and seizing him by the throat, he said, "Pay what you owe." Then his fellow slave fell down and pleaded with him, "Have patience with me, and I will pay you." But he refused; then he went and threw him into prison until he would pay the debt.

When his fellow slaves saw what had happened, they were greatly distressed, and they went and reported to their lord all that had taken place. Then his lord summoned him and said to him, "You wicked slave! I forgave you all that debt because you pleaded with me. Should you not have had mercy on your fellow slave, as I had mercy on you?" And in anger his lord handed him over to be tortured until he would pay his entire debt. So my heavenly Father will also do to every one of you, if you do not forgive your brother or sister from your heart.

Mt 18:23-35

Interpretation: In the realm of heaven forgiveness begets forgiveness. You are greatly indebted to God, not only for your iniquities against creation, but for the myriad blessings that you have received. You are indebted beyond your means to ever repay, but God forgives you without condition and does not ask you for repayment. When you emanate divine compassion and loving kindness, and forgive those who are indebted to you, you not only free them from their bondage to you, you also free yourself. No longer are you tortured by the stress, anxiety, and anger that you feel when you hold something against another. When you forgive from your heart you are truly free.

The Weeds among the Wheat

The kingdom of heaven may be compared to someone who sowed good seed in his field; but while everybody was asleep, an enemy came and sowed weeds among the wheat, and then went away. So when the plants came up and bore grain, then the weeds appeared as well. And the slaves of the householder came and said to him, "Master, did you not sow good seed in your field? Where then, did these weeds come from?" He answered, "An enemy has done this." The slaves said to him, "Then do you want us to go and gather them?" But he replied, "No; for in gathering the weeds you would uproot the wheat along with them. Let both of them grow together until the harvest; and at the harvest time I will tell the reapers, Collect the weeds first and bind them in bundles to be burned, but gather the wheat into my barn.

Mt 13:24-30

Interpretation: In the realm of heaven you reap what you sow. You may live your life trying to be good and to do the right thing in the hope that you are living an exemplary life, but suddenly you discover that you are also capable of entangling your life in undesirable ways. This happens when you have been living unconsciously. Your may consider it the work of an external enemy, but, in fact, it is sabotage from within. You may be tempted to simply uproot the unwanted part of yourself and rid yourself of it. But living consciously you realize that you cannot uproot what is a part of you without also destroying all of you. Instead of destroying the part of you that you don't want, embrace it. Recognize it as part of who you are and remain conscious of it lest it increase and overtake you when you least expect it. When you are living consciously, even the part of you that you consider undesirable can be beneficial if you pay attention to it and learn from it.

The Leaven

The kingdom of heaven is like yeast that a woman took and mixed in with three measures of flour until all of it was leavened.

Mt 13:33-35

Interpretation: Once you are conscious of the realm of heaven, you are dramatically transformed. Your flat, mundane life rises to a more excellent way of living, and you offer yourself up as nourishment for the world. The realm of heaven expands your soul, and consequently every soul you touch.

The Mustard Seed

The kingdom of heaven is like a mustard seed that someone took and sowed in his field; it is the smallest of all the seeds, but when it has grown it is the greatest of shrubs and becomes a tree, so that the birds of the air come and make nests in its branches.

Mt 13:31-32

Interpretation: The seed of God is sown into your soul, conceiving the realm of heaven. It begins small and seems insignificant at its inception, but grows steadily within you until it becomes your whole life. Rooted in humanity and infused with divinity, the realm of heaven grows to great significance and stature as a font of refreshment and restoration for the world.

The Net

Again, the kingdom of heaven is like a net that was thrown into the sea and caught fish of every kind; when it was filled, they drew it ashore, sat down, and put the good into baskets but threw out the bad. So it will be at the end of the age. The angels will come out and separate the evil from the righteous and throw them into the furnace of fire, where there will be weeping and gnashing of teeth.

Mt 13:47-50

Interpretation: You are loved and accepted by God just as you are. God penetrates your unconscious and gathers up the good and the bad within you, bringing it all into consciousness. There, the angels of your higher self help you to choose a more excellent way to live by preserving the good in you and converting the bad into energy for the promulgation of the realm of heaven. There is grief and consternation as you release what works against you and embrace what makes you whole.

The Pearl

Again, the kingdom of heaven is like a merchant in search of fine pearls; on finding one pearl of great value, he went and sold all that he had and bought it.
Mt 13:45

Interpretation: As you search for the finer things of life which you believe will make you happy, you find the finest thing of all — the realm of heaven. It has the greatest value and can be had only at great cost. To claim the realm of heaven as your own, you must exchange all that you have for it, holding nothing back.

Other Parables of Jesus

Parables are more than just illustrations that support a principle. They are stories based on real life that stimulate the conscience of the listener and illicit a response from the heart. Jesus would say to the crowds who followed him, "Let anyone with ears listen" (Mt 11:15)! He knew that the ear and the heart were essential for the parable to work.

The Prodigal Son

There was a man who had two sons. The younger of them said to his father, "Father, give me the share of the property that will belong to me." So he divided his property between them. A few days later the younger son gathered all he had and traveled to a distant country and there he squandered his property in dissolute living. When he had spent everything, a severe famine took place throughout that country, and he began to be in need. So he went and hired himself out to one of the citizens of that country, who sent him to his fields to feed the pigs. He would gladly have filled himself with the pods that the pigs were eating; and no one gave him anything. But when he came to himself he said, "How many of my father's hired hands have bread enough and to spare, but here I am dying of hunger! I will get up and go to my father, and will say to him, 'Father, I have sinned against heaven and before you; I am no longer worthy to be called your son; treat me like one of your hired hands.'" So he set off and went to his father. But while he was still far off, his father saw him and was filled with compassion; he ran and put his arms around him and kissed him. Then the son said to him, "Father, I have sinned against heaven and before you; I am no longer worthy to be called your son." But the father said to his slaves, "Quickly, bring out a robe – the best one – and put it on him; put a ring on his finger and sandals on his feet. And get the fatted calf and kill it, and let us eat and celebrate; for this son of mine was dead and is alive again; he was lost and is found!" and they began to celebrate.

Interpretation: You can neither earn the loving presence of God nor escape it. Believe in the constant love, compassion, and forgiveness of God. You have inherited the realm of heaven and you will not go wanting. Yet, sometimes you take it upon yourself to venture away from God, believing in your self-sufficiency and independence. You rebel against what you believe is expected of you and you waste what has been given you, all in the name of freedom. You soon discover that your irresponsibility and prodigality do not lead to freedom after all. In fact, a life dedicated solely to what you want ends up in disappointment and disillusionment. Your journey to the land of enchantment takes you from one mirage to another until you arrive at the land of disenchantment, empty of purse and purpose, longing for that which you took for granted. Separated from God, you may be surviving, but you are not living.

Your hunger for adventure and novelty gives way to your hunger for God. With nothing left to lose, you are truly free to choose. Choose to change your conception of God. Choose to change the way you experience life. Choose to be transformed from one who is entitled to one who deserves nothing; from one who wants to be filled to one who is now empty; from one who would be served to one prepared to serve. In this moment of awakening remember who you are. You are a child of God. You arise from death and come alive once more. No longer lost, you find your way back home. Even before you arrive, God comes forth to welcome you. Even before you ask forgiveness for your debauchery, you've already been forgiven. It would be just for you to be penalized for your carousel, yet you receive a royal treatment. It would be expected for you to face some ostracism, yet you are met with a compassionate embrace. It would make sense for you to be required to earn back your familial place, yet you are escorted into the heart of God.

The Prodigal Son (continued)

Now his elder son was in the field; and when he came and approached the house, he heard music and dancing. He called one of the slaves and asked what was going on. He replied, "Your brother has come, and your father has killed the fatted calf, because he has got him back safe and sound." Then he became angry and refused to go in. His father came out and began to plead with him. But he answered his father, "Listen! For all these years I have been working like a slave for you, and I have never disobeyed your command; yet you have never given me even a young goat so that I might celebrate with my friends. But when this son of yours came back, who has devoured your property with prostitutes; you killed the fatted calf for him!" Then the father said to him, "Son, you are always with me, and all that is mine is yours.

But we had to celebrate and rejoice, because this brother of yours was dead and has come to life; he was lost and has been found."

Lk 15:11-32

Interpretation: Sometimes your transgression is not that you leave the presence of God, but that you remain for the wrong reasons. Behaving well and following rules and commandments is not enough. Being faithful and obedient in order to stay in God's good graces is an attempt to earn the loving presence of God, but you cannot earn it. When you expect to be rewarded for being good you are merely transacting business. Rather than pursue reciprocation from God, love God above all else and live your life in accordance with that love. Live for God alone, with no expectations of reward or punishment; remain with God for the sake of God. Be willing to lose your autonomous self in order to be one with God; and die to self-concernment that you may live for God alone.

The Lost Sheep

Take care that you do not despise one of these little ones; for, I tell you, in heaven their angels continually see the face of my Father in heaven. What do you think? If a shepherd has a hundred sheep, and one of them has gone astray, does he not leave the ninety-nine on the mountain and go in search of the one that went astray? And if he finds it, truly I tell you, he rejoices over it more than over the ninety-nine that never went astray. So it is not the will of your Father in heaven that one of these little ones should be lost.

Mt 18:10-14

Interpretation: All souls are precious in the eyes of God. Those who are lost are as important to the realm of heaven as those who have not strayed. The spirit of God will search for the soul that is lost until it is found and brought home where it belongs.

The Wedding Guest

When you are invited by someone to a wedding banquet, do not sit down at the place of honor, in case someone more distinguished than you has been invited by your host; and the host who invited both of you may come and say to you, "Give this person your place," and then in disgrace you would start to take the lowest place. But when you are invited, go and sit down at the lowest place, so that when your host comes, he may say to you, "Friend, move up higher;" then you will be honored in the presence of all who sit at the table with you. For all who exalt themselves will be humbled, and those who humble themselves will be exalted.

Lk 14:7-11

Interpretation: You have your place and that place is at the confluence of heaven and earth. Though you fly on eagles' wings, you need to be grounded; though you are tended by angels, you are a servant to the world. You, who put on external trappings of importance, are unaware of your intrinsic value as a being of God. You, who are prideful and arrogant, hide the shame you feel within. To exalt yourself is to set yourself up for a great and humiliating fall. Self-aggrandizement cannot stand up to the scrutiny of time. God alone assigns you your place under the sun.

The Faithful Servant

Who then is the faithful and prudent manager whom his master will put in charge of his slaves, to give them their allowance of food at the proper time? Blessed is the slave whom his master will find at work when he arrives. Truly I tell you, he will put that one in charge of all his possessions. But if that slave says to himself, "My master is delayed in coming," and if he begins to beat the other slaves, men and women, and to eat and drink and get drunk, the master of that slave will come on a day when he does not expect him and at an hour that he does not know, and will cut him in pieces, and put him with the unfaithful. That slave who knew what his master wanted, but did not prepare himself or do what was wanted, will receive a severe beating. But the one who did not know and did what deserved a beating will receive a light beating. From everyone to whom much has been given, much will be required; and from the one to whom much has been entrusted, even more will be demanded.

Lk 12:42-48

Interpretation: Faithfulness is not contingent on reward or punishment, but is constant regardless of the presence or absence of oversight. Faithfulness is by definition reliable and trustworthy and needs no direct supervision. Love God and live according to God's will without thought of credit or demerit.

If you know the will of God and ignore it, the cost is high. In order to disobey the will of God you have to close off your heart to God and this self-imposed exile is hell. If you do not know the will of God and therefore don't do it, it still hurts you because it is a sign that you are not in accord with God. If you are given the clarity of mind to discern the will of God, and the courage of heart to carry it out, then you are asked for even more. If you are trusted by God to attend to your own life and you do it faithfully, then God charges you with even more – the responsibility to foster and promulgate the divine essence in the world.

The Grateful King

Then the king will say to those at his right hand, "Come, you that are blessed by my Father, inherit the kingdom prepared for you from the foundation of the world; for I was hungry and you gave me food, I was thirsty and you gave me something to drink, I was a stranger and you welcomed me, I was naked and you gave me clothing, I was sick and you took care of me, I was in prison and you visited me." Then the righteous will answer him, "Lord, when was it that we saw you hungry and gave you food, or thirsty and gave you something to drink? And when was it that we saw you a stranger and welcomed you, or naked and gave you clothing? And when was it that we saw you sick or in prison and visited you?" And the king will answer them, "Truly I tell you, just as you did it to one of the least of these who are members of my family, you did it to me."

Mt 25:34-40

Interpretation: Enter, you whom are sanctified by God, for the realm of heaven has been yours from the beginning. It was you who had compassion on me and responded to my needs. You did not know me, yet you treated me as you would a friend. Without a thought of compensation, you came to me in the name of love. Every time you reached out to help someone in need, you did it to me. Every time you were kind to a stranger or smiled at a child, you did it to me. Every time you shared your bounty with the poor, and every time you acted compassionately toward the sick, the abandoned, and the lost, you did it to me. And every time you did it to me, you did it to God.

The Fig Tree

A man had a fig tree planted in his vineyard; and he came looking for fruit on it and found none. So he said to the gardener, "See here! For three years I have come looking for fruit on this fig tree, and still I find none. Cut it down! Why should it be wasting the soil?" He replied, "Sir, let it alone for one more year, until I dig around it and put manure on it. If it bears fruit next year, well and good; but if not, you can cut it down."

Lk 13:6-9

Interpretation: You are given life to be fruitful in the world, but for some of you it takes a little longer than others to bear fruit. It is easy for you to lose patience with your life during the dry and barren season. You feel worthless and nonproductive. You judge your life as useless and good for naught, deserving elimination. Yet God pleads with you for patience and forgiveness. God refuses to give up on you, believing instead in your inherent capacity for spiritual awakening. Through transformation new life is possible. God knows that with some care and tending your soul will eventually flourish. God wants to till the soil of your earthy life so that you may more readily receive the gift of nourishment. God wants to prune away the parts of you that have already died, and make room for the life that is to come. God wants to make fertile your soul that you may bear the fruit of heaven, which is love.

The Shrewd Manager

There was a rich man who had a manager, and charges were brought to him that this man was squandering his property. So he summoned him and said to him,

"What is this that I hear about you? Give me an accounting of your management, because you cannot be my manager any longer." Then the manager said to himself, "What will I do, now that my master is taking the position away from me? I am not strong enough to dig, and I am ashamed to beg. I have decided what to do so that, when I am dismissed as manager, people may welcome me into their homes." So, summoning his master's debtors one by one, he asked the first, "How much do you owe my master?" He answered, "A hundred jugs of olive oil." He said to him, "Take your bill, sit down quickly, and make it fifty." Then he asked another, "And how much do you owe?" He replied, "A hundred containers of wheat." He said to him, "Take your bill and make it eighty." And his master commended the dishonest manager because he had acted shrewdly; for the children of this age are more shrewd in dealing with their own generation than are the children of the light. And I tell you, make friends for yourselves by means of dishonest wealth so that when it is gone, they may welcome you into the eternal homes.

Whoever is faithful in a very little is faithful also in much; and whoever is dishonest in a very little is dishonest also in much. If then you have not been faithful with the dishonest wealth, who will entrust to you the true riches? And if you have not been faithful with what belongs to another, who will give you what is your own?

Lk 16:1-12

Interpretation: Even if you have not been a good steward of the life that has been entrusted to you, and even if your dishonesty has alienated you from God, it is not too late for you. In your hour of truth, in the midst of your spiritual crisis, invoke the wisdom of your soul. When you are faced with a choice between temporal and eternal security, choose the latter. At your core, you have a keen awareness of the difference between the ephemeral and the everlasting. Regardless of your weaknesses and limitations, your passionate longing for your eternal home compels you to act wisely and boldly to reunite yourself with God. The same cunning you have used to obtain material wealth you can use to obtain spiritual wealth. Shrewdness and practicality can be used in the service of God. Be perceptive of the reality around you so that you avoid building your life on sand, and do the will of God. You remain true to your propensity toward honesty or dishonesty whether you are dealing with minor or major matters, yet, in your shrewdness devote yourself to God alone and commit to serve God above all else.

The Rich Fool

The land of a rich man produced abundantly. And he thought to himself, "What should I do, for I have no place to store my crops?" Then he said, "I will do this: I will pull down my barns and build larger ones, and there I will store all my grain and my goods. And I will say to my soul, Soul, you have ample goods laid up for many years; relax, eat, drink, be merry." But God said to him, "You fool! This very night your life is being demanded of you. And the things you have prepared, whose will they be?" So it is with those who store up treasures for themselves but are not rich toward God.

Lk 12:16-21

Interpretation: Your life consists not in what you possess, but in what possesses you. More important than having goods in reserve is having the love of God in your heart. Your covetousness distracts you from the greatest security of all – your abidance in God. God provides you with what you need. Share with others what you receive and do not hoard it today for fear of tomorrow. It is foolish for you to take longevity for granted. Guard against greed that accumulates more than you need for the present, and against fear that makes you stockpile for the future.

A House Divided

How can Satan cast out Satan? If a kingdom is divided against itself, that kingdom cannot stand. And if a house is divided against itself, that house will not be able to stand. And if Satan has risen up against himself and is divided, he cannot stand, but his end has come.

Mk 3:23-26

Interpretation: Evil does not turn on evil lest it destroy itself. Do not confuse the power of good with the power of evil, whose only power derives from the absence of God consciousness.

Overcoming Evil

But no one can enter a strong man's house and plunder his property without first tying up the strong man; then indeed the house can be plundered.

Mk 3:27

Interpretation: Only by inhibiting the power of evil by the power of God consciousness can evil be overcome.

The Friend at Midnight

Suppose one of you has a friend, and you go to him at midnight and say to him, "Friend, lend me three loaves of bread; for a friend of mine has arrived, and I have nothing to set before him." And he answers from within, "Do not bother me; the door has already been locked, and my children are with me in bed; I cannot get up and give you anything." I tell you, even though he will not get up and give him anything because he is his friend, at least because of his persistence he will get up and give him whatever he needs.

Lk 11:5-10

Interpretation: When you seek God in your heart, when you knock to be heard, and when you ask for what you need, God cannot help but respond to your plea. God gives you what you need, not because you deserve it, but because you are sincere in your prayer. Turn to God unabashedly regardless of the hour and in spite of the circumstances in which you find yourself. Turn to God believing that God will provide what you need. Know that you will not be judged for your indigence or shunned for your utter dependence on God.

The Two Debtors

A certain creditor had two debtors; one owed five hundred denarii, and the other fifty. When they could not pay, he canceled the debts for both of them. Now which of them will love him more?

Lk 7:41-43

Interpretation: Love begets forgiveness and forgiveness begets love. Because God loves you, you are forgiven not only of your smallest transgressions against heaven and earth, but also of your most grievous. Your natural response to such forgiveness is gratitude, humility, and love. The more you are forgiven, the greater your love. Then your love begets your forgiveness of others, and the circle of love continues.

Lazarus

There was a rich man who was dressed in purple and fine linen and who feasted sumptuously every day. And at his gate lay a poor man named Lazarus, covered with sores, who longed to satisfy his hunger with what fell from the rich man's table; even the dogs would come and lick his sores. The poor man died and was carried away by the angels to be with Abraham. The rich man also died and was buried. In Hades, where he was being tormented, he looked up and saw Abraham far away with Lazarus by his side. He called out, "Father Abraham, have mercy on me, and send Lazarus to dip the tip of his finger in water and cool my tongue; for I am in agony in these flames." But Abraham said, "Child, remember that during your lifetime you received your good things, and Lazarus in like manner evil things; but now he is comforted here, and you are in agony. Besides all this, between you and us a great chasm has been fixed, so that those who might want to pass from here to you cannot do so, and no one can cross from there to us." He said, "Then, father, I beg you to send him to my father's house – for I have five brothers – that he may warn them, so that they will not also come into this place of torment." Abraham replied, "They have Moses and the prophets; they should listen to them." He said, "No, Father Abraham; but if someone goes to them from the dead they will repent." He said to him, "If they do not listen to Moses and the prophets, neither will they be convinced even if someone rises from the dead."

Lk 16:19-31

Interpretation: To disdain or reject any part of yourself brings disunion to the whole, and casts you into the torment of separation. On the one hand, you are ready to honor and celebrate the part of you of which you are proud, and you do not hesitate to nurture that part and to treat it royally. The part of you that you are eager to acknowledge wants for nothing. You give it your attention, your possessions, and your high esteem. This part can become arrogant and self-indulgent; it can be

44

self-absorbed, and indifferent to all else. On the other hand, you deny or ignore the part of yourself that is humble, patient, and is grateful to receive even the smallest of gifts. You consider that part of you weak and needy. You are either ashamed of that part of yourself or oblivious to it. In effect, you starve that part of yourself through inattention and neglect. You create a chasm within you that cannot be bridged.

When you suddenly find yourself without the trappings that have defined you and the hubris that has held you aloft, you come to the sinking realization that you have rejected the cornerstone of your being. It becomes clear to you that you have embraced the temporal part of yourself and have scorned the everlasting. Sometimes it takes a descent into the pit of desolation and the agony of separation to realize the extent of your self-discrimination. Only then do you acknowledge your basic need to integrate all parts of yourself into the whole person who God has made you.

Reverse the disunion you have brought upon the whole. Bridge the gulf you have created between the parts of you. Words alone cannot bring about wholeness, and reaching out to bring the parts together is futile. The only way to reconcile the parts of the whole, the only way to bridge the chasm, is to love yourself in totality. Then you realize that the part of yourself that you have rejected, God elevates; and the part of yourself that you have cast aside, God enriches.

The Good Samaritan

A man was going down from Jerusalem to Jericho, and fell into the hands of robbers, who stripped him, beat him, and went away, leaving him half dead. Now by chance a priest was going down that road; and when he saw him, he passed by on the other side. So likewise a Levite, when he came to the place and saw him, passed by on the other side. But a Samaritan while traveling came near him; and when he saw him, he was moved with pity. He went to him and bandaged his wounds, having poured oil and wine on them. Then he put him on his own animal, brought him to an inn, and took care of him. The next day he took out two denarii, gave them to the innkeeper, and said, "Take care of him; and when I come back, I will repay you whatever more you spend. Which of these three, do you think, was a neighbor to the man who fell into the hands of the robbers? Lk 10:30-36

Interpretation: Every human being is your neighbor. No matter the time or distance that separates one human being from another, all souls are adjoined, connected and indivisible. When one is mistreated or falls into bad times, all are hurt. Even those with whom you have little in common or who are very different from you physically, culturally, or religiously, are your neighbors. When you are grounded in your humanity you care what happens to your neighbors and you are moved by love and compassion to help them. Sometimes, however, you may be more concerned with complying with religious requirements and fulfilling doctrinal expectations than you are about those in your midst who suffer. You may place political and ecclesiastical law above mercy, but the highest law is the law of love. This law is not to be found in the statutes or the Canons, but in the nature of the human soul. With love and compassion you overcome your fear, your prejudice, and your apathy. With love and compassion you tend to the wounded body, soothe the broken heart, and feed the destitute beggar. Love seeks no compensation but is its own reward. Compassion emanates from the profound understanding that we are all one.

The Wise and Foolish Builders

Everyone then who hears these words of mine and acts on them will be like a wise man who built his house on rock. The rain fell, the floods came, and the winds blew and beat on that house, but it did not fall, because it had been founded on rock. And everyone who hears these words of mine and does not act on them will be like a foolish man who built his house on sand. The rain fell, and the floods came, and the winds blew and beat against that house, and it fell – and great was its fall.
Mt 7:24-27

Interpretation: Go deep below the surface of your life and ground yourself in God. Listen to the words that are spoken in your heart and heed them. They will keep you safe and sound through times of turmoil and strife. To trust your soul to that which shifts and changes is foolish; but to trust it to that which is foundational and everlasting is wise.

The Unclean Spirit

When the unclean spirit has gone out of a person, it wanders through waterless regions looking for a resting place, but it finds none. Then it says, "I will return to my house from which I came." When it comes, it finds it empty, swept, and put in order. Then it goes and brings along seven other spirits more evil than itself, and they enter and live there; and the last state of that person is worse than the first. So it will be also with this evil generation.

Mt 12:43-45

Interpretation: Nature abhors a vacuum, even in your soul. It is not enough to be against a certain way of life; you must also be for a certain way of life. If you are emptied of the forces of malice and yet are not filled with the spirit of God, the malicious power returns even stronger than before. Only divine essence can keep malevolent interlopers at bay. This is true of individuals and of society as a whole.

The Lost Coin

Or what woman having ten silver coins, if she loses one of them, does not light a lamp, sweep the house, and search carefully until she finds it? When she has found it, she calls together her friends and neighbors, saying, "Rejoice with me, for I have found the coin that I had lost." Just so, I tell you, there is joy in the presence of the angels of God over one sinner who repents."

Lk 15:8-10

Interpretation: You are born whole, but you may lose parts of yourself as you venture through the darkened passages of life. When a part of you is lost, the whole is incomplete. Your soul will not rest until it has recovered the part of you that has gone missing. Its quest is vehement and thorough. It searches in the darkest and deepest regions of your being. It prompts your consciousness to chase away the shadows, and focus single-heartedly on the hunt for that which completes you. What exuberance overtakes your soul when the lost has been found! What joy it shares with God when the integral part returns!

The Sower

Listen! A sower went out to sow. And as he sowed, some seeds fell on the path, and the birds came and ate them up. Other seeds fell on rocky ground, where they did not have much soil, and they sprang up quickly, since they had no depth of soil. But when the sun rose, they were scorched; and since they had no root, they withered away. Other seeds fell among thorns, and the thorns grew up and choked them. Other seeds fell on good soil and brought forth grain, some a hundredfold, some sixty, some thirty. Let anyone with ears listen.

Mt 13:3-9

Interpretation: God sows the seeds of life on your ground of being. The seeds are imbued with the spirit of God, but they need the deep and fertile soil of your humanity to gestate and become viable and fruitful life. The seeds are sown indiscriminately because life in the spirit is available to everyone. Some of you are prepared to receive the spirit and some are not. Some of you are simply too busy and live too superficially to allow the spirit to penetrate your life. Some of you have hardened your heart in order to protect yourselves. Your rough and shallow exterior prevents you from fathoming the secrets of life that God wants to share. Without depth of understanding and with no roots to ground them in your soul, the seedlings of the spirit are left vulnerable to the elements and soon scorch and wither away. Some of you are burdened with habits, fears, distractions, prejudices, doubts, and desires that kill off potential life even as it is offered to you. Some of you have tilled the soil of your humanity with prayer and meditation. Your heart is open and receptive to the gift of God and you offer to God your fecundity. You understand that the seeds must die to bring forth the fruits of the spirit. But it is not enough to receive the seeds of God; you must be prepared to nurture them in your soul until new life bursts forth into the world.

The Wicked Tenants

Listen to another parable. There was a landowner who planted a vineyard, put a fence around it, dug a wine press in it, and built a watchtower. Then he leased it to tenants and went to another country. When the harvest time had come, he sent his slaves to the tenants to collect his produce. But the tenants seized his slaves and beat one, killed another, and stoned another. Again he sent other slaves, more than the first; and they treated them in the same way. Finally he sent his son to them saying, "They will respect my son." But when the tenants saw the son, they said to themselves, "This is the heir; come, let us kill him and get his inheritance." So they seized him, threw him out of the vineyard, and killed him. Now the owner of the vineyard comes, what will he do to those tenants? They (the disciples) said to him (Jesus), "He will put those wretches to a miserable death, and lease the vineyard to other tenants who will give him the produce at the harvest time." Jesus said to them, "Have you never read in the scriptures: 'The stone that the builders rejected has become the cornerstone; this was the Lord's doing, and it is amazing in our eyes'? Therefore I tell you, the kingdom of God will be taken away from you and given to a people that produces the fruit of heaven. The one who falls on this stone will be broken to pieces and it will crush anyone on whom it falls.

Mt 21:33-44

Interpretation: God grants you life with the expectation that you will live it to the fullest. You are given all that you need to protect yourself from external threats, and you are given vigilance lest you be sabotaged from without. All that is asked of you in return is that you use that with which you have been entrusted for the sake of God and God's creation. You are to share the fruits of your labor. Some of you, however, are sabotaged from within. You forget that all you have is from God. You fall into the delusion that you own your life and are self-sufficient and independent of God. You want to live your life for your own sake only. You even ignore or beat away the angels of your higher nature which remind you of your indebtedness to God. In your attempt to claim total proprietorship of your life you try to kill off and expel the spirit of God from your life. But your life cannot be fruitful or even survive if it is not rooted in the realm of heaven. Those of you who deny your utter dependence and holy obligation to God suffer greatly as a result of your belief. What you reject is offered to others who take it, work it, and share from its fruits. What you reject for yourself becomes for others the foundation of their life.

The Unjust Judge

In a certain city there was a judge who neither feared God nor had respect for people. In that city there was a widow who kept coming to him and saying, "Grant me justice against my opponent." For a while he refused; but later he said to himself, "Though I have no fear of God and no respect for anyone, yet because this widow keeps bothering me, I will grant her justice, so that she may not wear me out by continually coming." Listen to what the unjust judge says. And will not God grant justice to his chosen ones who cry to him day and night? Will he delay long in helping them? I tell you, he will quickly grant justice to them. And yet, when the Son of Man comes, will he find faith on earth?

Lk 18:1-8

Interpretation: If you can obtain justice from a faithless and disrespectful world, how much more will justice be yours from God who hears your plea even in the night, and responds to you with swiftness? Nevertheless, you must prepare the soil of your heart to receive it.

The Pharisee and Tax Collector

Two men went up to the temple to pray; one a Pharisee and the other a tax collector. The Pharisee, standing by himself, was praying thus, "God, I thank you that I am not like the other people: thieves, rogues, adulterers, or even like this tax collector. I fast twice a week; I give a tenth of all my income." But the tax collector, standing far off, would not even look up to heaven, but was beating his breast saying, "God, be merciful to me, a sinner!" I tell you, this man went down to his home justified rather than the other; for all who exalt themselves will be humbled, but all who humble themselves will be exalted.

Lk 18:9-14

Interpretation: You cannot make yourself right with God by your behavior alone. No matter how strictly you adhere to the dictates of your religion or fulfill what you believe to be the requirements of God, you do not have the power of self-sanctification. When you try to earn God's love and forgiveness you are living under the illusion of self-sufficiency. Do not attribute the grace and mercy of God to your virtuous living and spiritual attainment. Do not believe that you actually deserve what you receive from God because of your righteousness. It is foolish enough to boast to others of your acquired worthiness, but quite absurd to boast to God of your spiritual bona fides. What matters most in the realm of God is not how you have acted for or against God and God's creation, but whether or not you see yourself through the eyes of God. Realize in your humility just how precious you are to God, regardless of your weaknesses. Understand how dependent you are on God, regardless of your strengths. It is your poverty of spirit, not your piety that prepares you for the realm of heaven. God seeks from you, not prescribed sacrifices, but unconditional mercy. With a repenting heart, you ask God for mercy. With a loving heart, God asks you for the same.

The Two Sons

What do you think? A man had two sons; he went to the first and said, Son, go and work in the vineyard today." He answered, "I will not;"but later he changed his mind and went. The father went to the second and said the same; and he answered, "I go, sir;" but he did not go. Which of the two did the will of his father?
Mt 21:28-32

Interpretation: The will of God is made known to you in your heart and it is your choice whether or not to do it. Sometimes you are quick to pledge your allegiance to the will of God, that is, until it is time to do it. Then your zeal falls away, your pledge is forgotten, and your obedience turns to disobedience. You choose not to do the will of God, but your own. Sometimes you are certain what the will of God is, but because it is not congruent with your will, you reject it as too demanding or unrealistic. Ultimately, however, because the will of God is known in your heart, you are not content until you go and do it. Being conscious of the realm of heaven you not only do the will of God, you also will the will of God.

The Talents

For it (the kingdom of heaven) is as if a man, going on a journey, summoned his slaves and entrusted his property to them; to one he gave five talents, to another two, to another one, to each according to his ability. Then he went away. The one who had received the five talents went off at once and traded with them, and made five more talents. In the same way, the one who had the two talents made two more talents. But the one who had received the one talent went off and dug a hole in the ground and hid his master's money. After a long time the master of those slaves came and settled accounts with them. Then the one who had received the five talents came forward, bringing five more talents, saying, "Master, you handed over to me five talents; see, I have made five more talents." His master said to him, "Well done, good and trustworthy slave; you have been trustworthy in few things, I will put you in charge of many things; enter into the joy of your master." And the one with the two talents also came forward, saying, "Master, you handed over to me two talents; see, I have made two more talents." His master said to him, "Well done, good and trustworthy slave; you have been trustworthy in a few things, I will put you in charge of many things; enter into the joy of your master." Then the one who had received the one talent also came forward, saying, "Master, I knew that you were a harsh man, reaping where you did not sow, and gathering where you did not scatter seed; so I was afraid, and I went and hid your talent in the ground. Here you have what is yours." But his master replied, "You wicked and lazy slave! You knew, did you, that I reap where I did not sow, and gather where I did not scatter? Then you ought to have invested my money with the bankers, and on my return I would have ten talents. For to all those who have, more will be given, and they will have an abundance; but from those who have nothing, even what they have will be taken away. As for this worthless slave, throw him into the outer darkness, where there will be weeping and gnashing of teeth.

Mt 25:14-30

Interpretation: Being conscious of the realm of heaven you work for God, not for yourself. You receive a unique gift from God and need to use it to the best of your ability in the service of God. The more substantial the gift you receive, the more substantial your contribution must be. How you use your gift needs to be based not on your fear of retribution, but on your love for God. You need to use what you have been given lest you lose it altogether. The magnitude of your gift does not matter as much as what you do with it on behalf of God. When you use well even the little with which you have been charged, you are entrusted by God with even greater responsibility. To love and serve God without reservation and in total abandon fulfills your human purpose and brings joy to the heart of God, a joy in which you share.

Chapter Three
Truly I Tell You

When Jesus began his teachings with the phrase, "Truly I tell you... (Mt 21:21)," he was essentially saying to his followers, "What I am about to tell you is my heart-felt belief." While Jesus sometimes referred to the sacred writings, what he proclaimed was based mostly on his deeply-abiding love for God and his personal experience of life.

The Beatitudes

With these words Jesus offered his followers more than the principles of goodness and piety; he offered them a more excellent way of life. He guided them to their full potential as human beings, not by teaching them what to do, but what to be.

Poverty

Blessed are the poor in spirit, for theirs is the kingdom of heaven.
                                                                    Mt 5:3

Interpretation: Joyful are you who know your truest need, your emptiness will be filled, and your brokenness will be mended. Joyful are you who depend so completely on the love of God to see you through the day; you are open, available, and receptive to the realm of heaven. You set aside the illusion of your self-sufficiency and embrace the reality of your spiritual indigence. With the surrender of your life comes the prevalence of God.

Grief

Blessed are those who mourn, for they will be comforted.
                                                                    Mt 5:4

Interpretation: Joyful are you who allow the pain of your loss to consume you, you will be given the courage to enter the dark night of separation, and you will find the strength to endure until the dawn. Joyful are you who accept the reality of impermanence, even as you must bid farewell.

Humility

Blessed are the meek, for they will inherit the earth.
                                                                    Mt 5:5

Interpretation: Joyful are you who acknowledge the truth about yourself. In your honesty you recognize your potential and your limitation. In your humility you accept yourself as you are. Your decision to drop away the masks you wear brings you the freedom to be yourself. When you are open to the world, the world is open to you.

Yearning for God

Blessed are those who hunger and thirst for righteousness, for they will be filled.
Mt 5:6

Interpretation: Joyful are you who yearn for the ways of God. You seek sustenance for your soul, and you thirst for the nectar of heaven. Your volition for the will of God releases you from the snare of other appetites and fills you with the spirit of God.

Forgiveness

Blessed are the merciful, for they will receive mercy.
Mt 5:7

Interpretation: Joyful are you who forgive from your heart. You pardon the debts of others and release them from your hold. Joyful are you who accept the mercy of God and are willing to pass it on.

Single-heartedness

Blessed are the pure in heart, for they will see God.
Mt 5:8

Interpretation: Joyful are you who allow the ecstasy of love to overwhelm your heart. You discover joy even in suffering because you see the face of God in everything. Joyful are you who are conscious of God above all else.

Peace

Blessed are the peacemakers, for they will be called children of God.
Mt 5:9

Interpretation: Joyful are you who find the pacifism of God even in the conflict of life. Your tranquility of soul does not depend on the external, but on the state of your essential self. You, a child of God, give to posterity the peace you have inherited.

Courage

Blessed are those who are persecuted for righteousness' sake, for theirs is the kingdom of heaven.
Mt 5:10

Interpretation: Joyful are you who dare to live according to the dictates of your heart, even in the face of opposition. Neither pain nor humiliation, neither bondage nor death, can sway you from what you believe. Joyful are you whose faith is placed in the realm of heaven.

Love Above All

It was more important for Jesus to love in the name of God than to adhere to the precepts of religion or the customs of the day. He called on his followers to change their hearts from legality to spirituality, from apathy to compassion, from vengeance to forgiveness, and from hatred to love. He taught them to be responsive to the dire needs of their fellow human beings because to him the suffering of one was the suffering of all since all are one.

You Shall Love

The first (commandment) is, "Hear, O Israel: the Lord our God, the Lord is one; you shall love the Lord your God with all your heart, and with all your soul, and with all your mind, and with all your strength." The second is this, "You shall love your neighbor as yourself." There is no other commandment greater than these.

Mk 12:29

Interpretation: The instinct of your soul is to love God with your whole being; and loving God is tantamount to loving yourself and all to whom God has given life. Give your wholehearted presence to your Beloved for that is the sign of adoration. Be mindful of God in every moment. Whatever your thoughts or your distractions may be, return to the realm of heaven. Commend your soul to God and devote your life to the service of love. Use your strength in the name of God; let it manifest in gentle ways and humble living, yet let it protect the weak ones and speak out for the dispossessed.

Love Your Enemies

You have heard that it was said, "You shall love your neighbor and hate your enemy." But I say to you, Love your enemies and pray for those who persecute you, so that you may be children of your Father in heaven; for he makes his sun rise on the evil and on the good, and sends rain on the righteous and the unrighteous. For if you love those who love you, what reward do you have? Do not even the tax collectors do the same? And if you greet only your brothers and sisters, what more are you doing than others? Do not even the Gentiles do the same? Be perfect, therefore, as your heavenly Father is perfect.

Mt 5:43-48

Interpretation: Love takes you beyond logic, beyond hate, beyond anger and resentment. It does not discriminate, judge, or limit itself to those who reciprocate your love. This all-inclusive love is the radical love of God loving through you. Open your heart to it.

Treatment of Others

In everything do to others as you would have them do to you; for this is the law and the prophets.

Mt 7:12

Interpretation: You are one with all living beings. What happens to them happens to you, and what happens to you happens to them. Therefore, treat others as if they were you. Show them the kindness, thoughtfulness, mercy, and compassion that you would want to receive from them. More than the law and more than the prophets, it is the way of love.

Judgment

Do not judge, so that you may not be judged. For with the judgment you make you will be judged, and the measure you give will be the measure you get. Why do you see the speck in your neighbor's eye, but do not notice the log in your own eye? Or how can you say to your neighbor, "Let me take the speck out of your eye," while the log is in your own eye? You hypocrite, first take the log out of your own eye, and then you will see clearly to take the speck out of your neighbor's eye.

Mt 7:1-5

Interpretation: To be just, your judgment must be applied inclusively. What is good for one is good for the other. Before you judge another examine your own life; tend to your own shortcomings even as you focus on the shortcomings of another.

Words

Listen and understand; it is not what goes into the mouth that defiles a person, but it is what comes out of the mouth that defiles.

Mt 15:10-11

Interpretation: Words have the power to encourage or discourage another. They can praise or criticize, build up or tear down, please or offend. The words you choose to speak reveal what is inside of you. With every word you utter to another you have an opportunity to offer healing peace. In every case, let what you say be filtered through your loving heart.

Reconciled Heart

You have heard that it was said to those of ancient times, "You shall not murder;" and "whoever murders shall be liable to judgment." But I say to you that if you are angry with a brother or sister, you will be liable to judgment; and if you insult a brother or sister, you will be liable to the council; and if you say, "You fool," you will be liable to the hell of fire. So when you are offering your gift at the altar, if you remember that your brother or sister has something against you, leave your gift there before the altar and go; first be reconciled to your brother and sister, and then come and offer your gift. Come to terms quickly with your accuser while you are on the way to court with him, or your accuser may hand you over to the judge, and the judge to the guard, and you will be thrown into prison. Truly I tell you, you will never get out until you have paid the last penny.

Mt 5:21-26

Interpretation: Resolve your differences with others; cast off your hostility and refrain from insolence; seek forgiveness from those whom you have offended. It is not enough to do no harm to others; offer them truce, then offer them friendship; and let your amicability be prompted not by fear of retribution, but by love. The peace you offer to the world is the gift you offer to God.

Forgiveness

For if you forgive others their trespasses, your heavenly Father will also forgive you; but if you do not forgive others, neither will your Father forgive your trespasses.

Mt 6:14

Interpretation: When you open your heart to forgive others for their offenses against you, your heart also opens to receive God's forgiveness for your offences. A closed heart, however, is incapable of giving or receiving forgiveness, even from God.

Little Ones

Take care that you do not despise one of these little ones; for, I tell you, in heaven their angels continually see the face of my Father in heaven.

Mt 18:10

Interpretation: Treat gently and with respect those who are simple, humble, and vulnerable, for they are precious in the eyes of God. You are appointed to care for those who cannot care for themselves. Let them know God's love through you.

Sharing With Others

Jesus was deeply affected by the suffering of others. He looked upon their poverty, sickness, and despair and his heart broke. He witnessed their spiritual imprisonment and mental confusion and his soul was troubled. He beheld the human condition and was moved to compassion. Social categories did not matter to him, but the essence of each person did. Every being was precious to him and each soul was sacrosanct.

Beyond the Commandments

You know the commandments: "You shall not commit adultery; You shall not murder; You shall not steal; You shall not bear false witness; Honor your father and mother. …There is still one thing lacking. Sell all that you own and distribute the money to the poor, and you will have treasure in heaven; then come, follow me.

Lk 18:20, 22

Interpretation: Go beyond obedience of religious laws, and transcend goodness. Let compassion overwhelm your heart. Share your possessions with the dispossessed; leave the comfortable and familiar and follow me into poverty of spirit where you will not want for anything. Detach yourself from that which has become a god to you, including any physical, emotional, or spiritual attachment.

Possessions

Take care! Be on your guard against all kinds of greed; for one's life does not consist in the abundance of possessions.

Lk 12:15

Interpretation: When you least expect it, greed infiltrates your best defenses and blinds you to the truth. It matters not how much you collect, but how you live your life. Be not a prisoner of your belongings; instead be generous with what you have. Be prudent, but do not save everything for a rainy day lest the rains come and wash it all away.

Giving and Receiving

Pay attention to what you hear; the measure you give will be the measure you get, and still more will be given to you. For those who have, more will be given; and from those who have nothing, even what they have will be taken away.

Mk 4:24-25

Interpretation: You are like an artesian well. The more you offer to the world, the more you receive from the depths of your soul. But those who hoard what they have, even the little they have will dry up and disappear.

Riches

Truly I tell you, it will be hard for a rich person to enter the kingdom of heaven. Again I tell you, it is easier for a camel to go through the eye of a needle than for someone who is rich to enter the kingdom of God.

Mt 19:23-24

Interpretation: Your consciousness of the realm of heaven diminishes as your obsession for possessions, pleasure, and power increases. It is not only your obsession for money and material goods that blocks the realm of heaven from your mind, but also your excessive attachment to anything at all. Be grateful for what you have been given and use it well, but never allow it to become paramount in your life.

Secret Charity

So whenever you give alms, do not sound a trumpet before you, as the hypocrites do in the synagogues and in the streets, so that they may be praised by others. Truly I tell you, they have received their reward. But when you give alms, do not let your left hand know what your right hand is doing, so that your alms may be done in secret; and your Father who sees will reward you.

Mt 6:2-4

Interpretation: What shall you have in return for your philanthropy? Shall it be recognition from others? Shall it be admiration, acclaim or credit? Examine the motive behind your charity. If it turns out to be pure generosity or profound compassion or simply your response to the needs of others, then you can afford to do it in the privacy of your heart.

Give What You Have

Truly I tell you, this poor widow has put in more than all those who are contributing to the treasury. For all of them have contributed out of their abundance; but she out of her poverty has put in everything she had, all she had to live on.

Mk 12:43-44

Interpretation: Who gives more of themselves: the man who gives ten of his one hundred dollars or the woman who gives two of her two dollars? He has given from his abundance and, however beneficial his gift may be, she has given far more in proportion to her means. The same is true of what you offer back to God. Do you give a measured portion of your life or do you give all you have to give?

Precious Human Beings

For Jesus, every human being was sacred. He did not consider anyone intrinsically bad; instead, he believed everyone was inherently godly because they were part of God's creation. He believed that there was a kernel of good within each person. Even when he encountered a wrongdoer, he believed in the sanctity of that person. He believed in the capacity of human beings to change for the better, and asked his followers to turn away from anything in their lives that did not promote wholeness.

Goodness

Why do you call me good? No one is good but God alone.

Mt 19:17

Interpretation: Your goodness is but a reflection of divine goodness. If goodness is to come through you it will be because you are conscious of God, centered on God, and open to God.

Passion for Life

You are the salt of the earth; but if salt has lost its taste, how can its saltiness be restored? It is no longer good for anything, but is thrown out and trampled underfoot.

Mt 5:13

Interpretation: You make a difference in the world. Your passion for life is indispensable to those in your midst. Yet, there are times when all seems empty and darkness overcomes you. How can your passion for life be restored? It is through rest and re-creation, prayer and meditation. After all, your passion for life is the force of God.

Light

You are the light of the world. A city built on a hill cannot be hid. No one after lighting a lamp puts it under the bushel basket, but on the lamp stand, and it gives light to all in the house. In the same way, let your light shine before others, so that they may see your good works and give glory to your Father in heaven.

Mt 5:14-16

Interpretation: Your essence illuminates the lives of others. Do not hide the radiance of your being. Show it to others that they may know God through you. Share your luminosity with those whose minds are caught in darkness.

Let the Children Come

Let the little children come to me, and do not stop them; for it is to such as these that the kingdom of heaven belongs.

Mt 19:14

Interpretation: Little children abide in the realm of heaven and invite us to enter there. They are not clever, but authentic; they are not powerful, but vulnerable; they are not discriminating, but accepting; and they are not guileful, but innocent. Little ones melt the hardened heart and give meaning to the cynical mind. Remember what it was like to be a child and then you will know how to live.

Justice

The faith of Jesus went beyond obedience of religious laws to an intimate relationship with God. God was the beloved of his soul, the essence of his existence, and the purpose of his life. In full surrender, he gave himself up that God could live and love through him. But although his mind was constantly with God, he was rooted in the reality of the world. He found God, not in doctrinal prescriptions or proscriptions, but in people, in nature, and in life. He sought justice, not in a book, but in the heart.

Oaths

Again, you have heard that it was said to those of ancient times, "You shall not swear falsely, but carry out the vows you have made to the Lord." But I say to you, Do not swear at all, either by heaven, for it is the throne of God, or by the earth, for it is his footstool, or by Jerusalem, for it is the city of the great King. And do not swear by your head, for you cannot make one hair white or black. Let your word be "Yes, Yes," or "No, No;" anything more than this comes from the evil one.

Mt 5:33-37

Interpretation: Let your word stand on its own. There is no need to underscore your assurances with oaths or solemn vows. If you are honest, your simple affirmation or negation will suffice. If you are dishonest, no amount of swearing by God or by anything held precious will be enough.

Love and Goodness is the Law

Suppose one of you has only one sheep and it falls into a pit on the sabbath; will you not lay hold of it and lift it out? How much more valuable is a human being than a sheep! So it is lawful to do good on the Sabbath.

Mt 12:11-12

Interpretation: Loving your fellow human beings is not restricted to certain days of the week, nor is serving them. The compassionate love of God ignores the calendar and focuses on the immediate need of the beloved. Can you do less?

Something Greater

Have you not read what David did when he and his companions were hungry? He entered the house of God and ate the bread of the Presence, which it was not lawful for him or his companions to eat, but only for the priests. Or have you not read in the law that on the sabbath the priests in the temple break the sabbath and yet are guiltless? I tell you, something greater than the temple is here. But if you had known what this means, "I desire mercy and not sacrifice," you would not have condemned the guiltless. For the Son of Man is lord of the Sabbath.

Mt 12:3-8

Interpretation: Responding to the basic needs of your fellow human beings is more important than any law. The real transgression is for you to ignore the hungry or bypass the afflicted. The compassion of God that moves in your heart is greater than the temple, the church, or the mosque. Mercy is the justice that comes of love. Ritualistic sacrifices offered in honor of God pale in contrast to forgiveness, forbearance, and amnesty.

Vengeance

You have heard that it was said, "An eye for an eye and a tooth for a tooth." But I say to you, Do not resist an evildoer. But if anyone strikes you on the right cheek, turn the other also; and if anyone wants to sue you and take your coat, give your cloak as well; and if anyone forces you to go one mile, go also the second mile. Give to everyone who begs from you, and do not refuse anyone who wants to borrow from you.

Mt 5:38-42

Interpretation: In your lifetime you will suffer at the hands of others, but rather than react to their mistreatment with vengeance, respond with assertive self-respect. Return injury with nonviolence, theft with generosity, force with willingness and malice with kindness. Let your reprisal be not measure for measure, but love for hate; pardon for injury; and peace for conflict.

Wholeness

Jesus' teachings were not meant to condemn wrongdoings or promote virtue; rather, he was simply sharing his experience of God with his followers. He did not teach philosophy, morality, or ethics. Instead his teachings were simple and grounded in the reality of earthly life. He focused on the real and practical issues that mattered to his followers. He did not teach religious doctrine, but a way of life that he had personally experienced. He showed his followers a path that would lead them to God.

Enlightenment

The light is the lamp of the body. So, if your eye is healthy, your whole body will be full of light; but if your eye is unhealthy, your whole body will be full of darkness. If then the light in you is darkness, how great is the darkness.

Mt 6:22-23

Interpretation: The light of God enters your soul through your conscience, which is your intuitive sense of right and wrong. If your conscience is sound, your soul will be enlightened, but if your conscience is unsound, your soul will be unenlightened, and a soul without light is surely dark.

The Cloak

No one sews a piece of unshrunk cloth on an old cloak, for the patch pulls away from the cloak, and a worse tear is made.

Mt 9:16

Interpretation: You cannot begin a new healthy life while clinging to your old dysfunctional life. The new life is incompatible with the old and pulls away from it, leaving you torn between two ways of life and unable to live either.

The Wineskins

Neither is new wine put into old wineskins, the skins burst, and the wine is spilled, and the skins are destroyed; but new wine is put into fresh wineskins, and so both are preserved.

Mt 9:17

Interpretation: The transformation of your consciousness has to be total and definite. Your life cannot contradict your faith. There must be congruence between your inner and outer self, lest one destroy the other. When you allow the spirit of God to give birth to you anew, it is left to you to cast away the old and enter wholeheartedly into the new.

Moral Cancer

If your hand or your foot causes you to stumble, cut it off and throw it away; it is better for you to enter life maimed or lame than to have two hands or two feet and to be thrown into the eternal fire. And if your eye causes you to stumble, tear it out and throw it away; it is better for you to enter life with one eye than to have two eyes and be thrown into the hell of fire.

Mt 18:8-9

Interpretation: Cut away from yourself whatever impedes your fullness of life. Only by severing that which putrefies you from within can you restore yourself to wholeness. It is better that you sacrifice the part for the sake of the whole than the other way around.

Faith

For truly I tell you, if you have faith the size of a mustard seed, you will say to this mountain, "Move from here to there," and it will move; and nothing will be impossible for you.

Mt 17:20

Interpretation: Faith is more than belief; it is an inner knowing, a certainty that cannot be denied. Even a little faith can produce tremendous results. What you hold to be true in your mind affects greatly what in reality will be. Even when your wholehearted faith does not change the reality before you, it changes how you respond to that reality.

Fear of Death

Do not fear those who kill the body but cannot kill the soul; rather fear him who can destroy both soul and body in hell. Are not two sparrows sold for a penny? Yet not one of them will fall to the ground apart from your Father. And even the hairs of your head are all counted. So do not be afraid; you are of more value than many sparrows.

Mt 10:28-31

Interpretation: Not unlike a mother who examines carefully every inch of her newborn's little body, God knows intimately and deems precious every aspect of your intricate being. Your body is vulnerable, but your soul is inviolate. Do not fear the death of your impermanent body; instead believe in the eternality of your soul.

Anxiety

Therefore I tell you, do not worry about your life, what you will eat or what you will drink, or about your body, what you will wear. Is not life more than food, and the body more than clothing? Look at the birds of the air; they neither sow nor reap nor gather into barns, and yet your heavenly Father feeds them. Are you not of more value than they? And can any of you by worrying add a single hour to your span of life? And why do you worry about clothing? Consider the lilies of the field, how they grow; they neither toil nor spin, yet I tell you, even Solomon in all his glory was not clothed like one of these. But if God so clothes the grass of the field, which is alive today and tomorrow is thrown into the oven, will he not much more clothe you – you of little faith? Therefore do not worry, saying, "What will we eat?" or "What will we drink?" or "What will we wear?" for it is the Gentiles who strive for all these things; and indeed your heavenly Father knows that you need all these things. But strive first for the kingdom of God and his righteousness, and all these things will be given to you as well. So do not worry about tomorrow, for tomorrow will bring worries of its own. Today's trouble is enough for today.

Mt 6:25-34

Interpretation: Your livelihood is of great importance. Seek subsistence and protection from the elements, care for yourself and for your family, but do not let your heart be troubled. Have faith that God works through you to provide all that you need. Though you must plan for tomorrow, do not let the future overwhelm you with anxiety. Instead, let your focus be on the present which is when your actions matter. Seek the realm of heaven in the moment before you and expect the rest to follow.

Merciful Healing

Those who are well have no need of a physician, but those who are sick. Go and learn what this means, "I desire mercy, not sacrifice." For I have come to call not the righteous but sinners.

Mt 9:12

Interpretation: Those who acknowledge their need for healing are healed. But there can be no healing for those who are oblivious to their affliction or who deny it altogether. The offering of sacrifices may placate the gods of jealousy and revenge, but it is forgiveness that heals the soul.

Treasure of the Heart

Do not store up for yourselves treasures on earth, where moth and rust consume and where thieves break in and steal; but store up for yourselves treasures in heaven, where neither moth nor rust consumes and where thieves do not break in and steal. For where your treasure is, there your heart will be also.

Mt 6:19-21

Interpretation: Do not cling to the impermanent; relinquish all that is temporal. Keep what lasts forever and hold fast to that which is eternal.

Determine what it is that you would give up last, for that is the treasure of your heart?

Public Piety

Beware of practicing your piety before others in order to be seen by them; for then you have no reward from your Father in heaven.

Mt 6:1

Interpretation: It is one thing to display publicly your devotion to God, quite another to commune intimately with God. The former is for show, the latter is for love. Let your prayer be the secret language between your soul and your Beloved.

Rest for Your Soul

Come to me, all you that are weary and are carrying heavy burdens, and I will give you rest. Take my yoke upon you, and learn from me; for I am gentle and humble in heart, and you will find rest for your souls. For my yoke is easy, and my burden is light.

Mt 11:28-30

Interpretation: Come away from your wearisome life; let God offer you repose. Share with God your burden and let God teach you gentle ways and humbleness of heart. Yoked with God your stress is lessened and your load is lightened. Be with God this moment and set your soul at ease.

Private Fasting

And whenever you fast, do not look dismal, like the hypocrites, for they disfigure their faces so as to show others that they are fasting. Truly I tell you, they have received their reward. But when you fast, put oil on your head and wash your face, so that your fasting may be seen not by others but by your Father who is in secret; and your Father who sees in secret will reward you.

Interpretation: If what you desire is others' approval, you might receive it by fasting publicly. But if what you want is to discipline your body, harness your mind and strengthen your spirit, do it privately. Fast above all from vainglory and let your sacrifice be known to God alone. It is, after all, for the sake of God that you care for yourself.

Become Childlike

Truly I tell you, unless you change and become like children, you will never enter the kingdom of heaven. Whoever becomes humble like this child is the greatest in the kingdom of heaven. Whoever welcomes one such child in my name welcomes me.
Mt 18:3-5

Interpretation: Let yourself become childlike; return to your simplicity and innocence, humility and authenticity; for this is the nature of the realm of heaven. Welcome forth the child that lives within you. It is the child of God, the hope for all humanity.

Beware

Jesus experienced strong emotions. When he beheld the face of a little child his heart melted before such innocence. When he looked upon a world of hate and apathy his heart became profoundly sad. Injustice infuriated Jesus. He abhorred that some people were taken advantage of by others. He especially detested it when the powerful oppressed the powerless, using religion to control them. Nothing exasperated Jesus as much as religious leaders who took advantage of believers by setting themselves up as the only channel to God, and by establishing prescribed rites and rituals in order to keep control over the people. He saw through to their motives which had much more to do with their own power and prestige, than with loving God. Jesus' teachings stirred his followers so profoundly that the civil and religious authorities pursued him as a revolutionary.

Trust but Verify

Beware of false prophets, who come to you in sheep's clothing but inwardly are ravenous wolves. You will know them by their fruits. Are grapes gathered from thorns, or figs from thistles? In the same way, every good tree bears good fruit. Every tree that does not bear good fruit is cut down and thrown into the fire. Thus you will know them by their fruits."

Mt 7:15-20

Interpretation: Trust must be earned. Look to the effects of a person's life. Remember, trustworthiness begets trust and goodness begets goodness. Keep away from those who are deceitful or harmful to your welfare. You may love and forgive them, but this does not necessitate entanglement with them.

Beware of Religious Hierarchy

Watch out, and beware of the yeast of the Pharisees and Sadducees.

Mt 16:6

Interpretation: Do not be mystified by those who don religious garments and puff up their importance. They are no more and no less than you. Place no one between you and God; allow for no liaison between you and your Beloved. A truly holy and humble guide will lead you to God then step aside and let you be.

Blind Guides

Every plant that my heavenly Father has not planted will be uprooted. Let them alone; they are blind guides of the blind. And if one blind person guides another, both will fall into a pit.

Mt 15:13

Interpretation: Let others sow their seeds of customs and traditions. With blind eyes they direct others and lead them toward an even greater blindness. Trust your heart to tell you what is important and what is not. Nothing lasts except what God plants in your heart.

Fruits of Consciousness

Therefore I tell you, the kingdom of God will be taken away from you and given to a people that produces the fruits of the kingdom.

Mt 21:43

Interpretation: You are given the realm of heaven. It is up to you to nurture this gift to fruition. Unless you do, you will lose it altogether. You are the laborer who is needed to harvest the yield of God. Let it be a labor of love.

Interpreting Signs

When it is evening, you say, "It will be fair weather, for the sky is red." And in the morning, "It will be stormy today, for the sky is red and threatening." You know how to interpret the appearance of the sky, but you cannot interpret the signs of the times. An evil and adulterous generation asks for a sign, but no sign will be given to it except the sign of Jonah.

Mt 16:2-4

Interpretation: How is it that you so easily interpret the signs of coming weather, but ignore the signs of what is before you now and, consequently, of that which is to come? Give attention to what you are doing now and consider the consequences of your actions. Pay heed to what is being allowed to happen in the world around you now and what will come of it. Be responsible, for tomorrow depends on today.

Chapter Four
Pray Always

The faith of Jesus went beyond the impersonal character of religious law to an intimate relationship with God. The God he knew most intimately was the one he encountered in prayer and meditation. He counseled his disciples to "Watch therefore and pray always…" (Lk 21:36).

Pray Then in This Way

In prayer Jesus gave himself up that God could live and love through him. He taught his disciples to do the same: "Pray then in this way…" (Mt 6:9).

In Secret

And whenever you pray, do not be like the hypocrites; for they love to stand and pray in the synagogues and at the street corners, so that they may be seen by others. Truly I tell you, they have received their reward. But whenever you pray, go into your room and shut the door and pray to your Father who is in secret; and your Father who sees in secret will reward you.

Mt 6:5-6

Interpretation: God is hidden in the depths of your being; therefore let your prayer be intimate and private, authentic and pure. What comes from your secret rendezvous with God is more sincere than from any public display.

With Sincerity

When you are praying, do not heap up empty phrases as the Gentiles do; for they think that they will be heard because of their many words. Do not be like them, for your Father knows what you need before you ask him.

Mt 6:7-8

Interpretation: Do not pray with a multitude of meaningless words; pray instead, believing that your innermost desires are already known by God. Remain with your Beloved in the silence of your mind and the stillness of your soul.

With Faith

Whatever you ask for in prayer with faith, you will receive.

Mt 21:22

Interpretation: When you pray with all your heart you open yourself to the ways of God. Your prayer becomes God's prayer in you. You will God's will, and think God's thoughts, and love with the heart of God. Pray, not so that God will know what you want; pray, rather, so that you can know what God wants.

It Will Be Done

Again, truly I tell you, if two of you agree on earth about anything you ask, it will be done for you by my Father in heaven. For where two or three are gathered in my name, I am there among you.

Mt 18:19-20

Interpretation: When you join with others on behalf of humanity, the spirit of God is with you and your united prayer impacts the deepest aspects of life. How many come together to pray is not as important as the unity that is formed among you.

Ask, Search, Knock

Ask and it will be given to you; seek and you will find; knock and the door will be opened for you. For everyone who asks receives, and everyone who searches finds, and for everyone who knocks, the door will be opened. Is there anyone among you who, if your child asks for bread, will give a stone? Or if the child asks for a fish, will give a snake? If you then, who are evil, know how to give good gifts to your children, how much more will your Father in heaven give good things to those who ask him.

Mt 7:7-11

Interpretation: God awaits your entreaty, your quest, and your readiness to receive the realm of heaven. It is God's nature to give, to reveal, and to open to you. Although you may not always know how to pray, your intention and attention is enough.

Keep Awake

Keep awake and pray that you may not come into the time of trial; the spirit indeed is willing, but the flesh is weak.

Mk 14:38

Interpretation: Only your fully-awakened consciousness can sustain you when passions of the flesh tempt you away from healthy living. Be present to the moment and pray without ceasing; pray to the spirit of God within you to embolden your resolve.

Jesus Prays

For Jesus, prayer was as necessary as breath. Deep within his soul he experienced unquenchable hunger and thirst to be with God. He would leave the crowd regularly to be alone in prayer. He would wander off to a desert place to find the silence and solitude his soul required; or he would climb a mountain and spend the night communing with God. Jesus communicated with God with reverent familiarity and open-hearted intimacy. Because he prayed privately in secluded places, we have only a few of his recorded prayers.

The Lord's Prayer

Our Father in heaven, hallowed be your name. Your kingdom come. Your will be done, on earth as it is in heaven. Give us this day our daily bread. And forgive us our debts, as we also have forgiven our debtors. And do not bring us to the time of trial, but rescue us from the evil one.

Mt 6:9-13

Interpretation: Beloved One who lives within us, cherished is your name. Your spirit comes and your love abounds on earth as in heaven. We survive day by day on your sustenance, but we thrive eternally on your presence. Your merciful way sets free our soul and we can do no less with those who owe us. You give us the strength to overcome temptation and the faith to withstand the darkness that comes upon us.

Revelation

I thank you, Father, Lord of heaven and earth, because you have hidden these things from the wise and the intelligent and have revealed them to infants; yes, Father, for such was your gracious will.

Lk 10:21

Interpretation: God of all creation, the secrets of the universe are not for all to know. You open the eyes of children, but blind the learned and the shrewd. You reveal your truth to those of simple faith and humble heart, while obscuring it to the clever and astute. Your grace alone unlocks your mysteries for those who reach for heaven, while standing firmly on the earth.

Remove this Cup

Abba, Father, for you all things are possible; remove this cup from me; yet not what I want, but what you want.

Mk 14:36

Interpretation: Holy Being, giver and protector of life, save me from the agony that awaits me. If there is another way…yet, if it has to be, let it serve your purpose. You do not will that I should suffer at the hands of others; you do not will that I should die. You will that I teach the world to love.

Forgive Them

Father, forgive them; for they do not know what they are doing.

Lk 23:34

Interpretation: God of Mercy, have mercy on those who do me harm. They do not realize that what they do to me they do to you and to themselves. They have yet to learn that we are one.

Forsaken

My God, my God, why have you forsaken me?

Mk 15:34

Interpretation: My Essence, my Life, why have you withdrawn your presence? Ground of my being, I am without foundation! The purpose of my existence is blurred and my mission seems of no avail! When will this dark night pass into the dawn? Be with me until the light.

Into Your Hands

Father, into your hands I commend my spirit.

Lk 23:46

In Essence: Creator of my life, I return to you from whom I've come. Even as the earth absorbs my flesh, I surrender my soul to you.

Chapter Five
Follow Me

Jesus never asked his disciples to worship or idolize him; he asked only to be followed. But to follow him meant losing themselves in something beyond anything they had ever known. Jesus' invitation was simple, "Follow me" (Mt 4:19).

Cost of Discipleship

How alluring is the call to be followers of Jesus, but to respond we must be willing to risk becoming vulnerable as we enter the unchartered waters of the soul.

As followers of Jesus, we are asked not to withdraw from the world, but to enter into it fully, carrying with us the power of love.

The call comes when we least expect it. We may be about our daily business, we may be in the midst of searching prayer, or we may be recreating ourselves in play and relaxation. Whether we hear it, see it, or sense it, the call is clear and undeniable. We are asked to stop doing what we are doing and change the direction of our life.

Follow Me

Follow me, and I will make you fish for people.

Mt 4:19

Interpretation: Come with me; I will draw your soul to God; and you will draw to God the souls of many. Be with me as I bring the love of God to all who are open to receive it. Help me to tend the wounded, heal the broken, and bring hope to the disenchanted. Follow me into the homes of the bereaved to offer comfort; into the crowds of hungry families to offer nourishment; and into the dens of iniquity to offer mercy and understanding.

Estimating the Cost

For which of you, intending to build a tower, does not first sit down and estimate the cost, to see whether he has enough to complete it? Otherwise, when he has laid a foundation and is not able to finish, all who see it will begin to ridicule him, saying, "This fellow began to build and was not able to finish." Or what king, going out to war against another king, will not sit down first and consider whether he is able with ten thousand to oppose one who comes against him with twenty thousand? If he cannot, then, while the other is still far away, he sends a delegation and asks for the terms of peace. So therefore, none of you can become my disciple if you do not give up all your possessions.

Lk 14:28-33

Interpretation: Do not commit to more than you can fulfill. First evaluate your resources and your willingness to stay the course no matter how difficult it might be. If you find that you do not possess the necessary resolve to take on the challenge, back away and acknowledge your limitations. Once committed, however, rid yourself of all encumbrances and follow me.

Proclaim the Good News

As you go proclaim the good news, "The kingdom of heaven has come near. Cure the sick, raise the dead, cleanse the lepers, cast out demons."

Mt 10:7-8

Interpretation: You have the power to bring others to wholeness through love. Reach out not only to those who are physically ill, but to those who are emotionally and spiritually broken. Call to life those who have died to the glory of their humanity. Renew in them the motivation to live abundantly and wholeheartedly. Welcome those who have been discarded by society; take the hand of the dejected ones; and ask forgiveness for those who have scorned them. Teach those who are shackled to destructive ways that it is by the power of God's love that they are set free. Tell them that the redeeming spirit of God sheds light on the worst of their shadows.

Wise and Innocent

See, I am sending you out like sheep into the midst of wolves; so be wise as serpents and innocent as doves. Beware of them, for they will hand you over to councils and flog you in their synagogues; and you will be dragged before governors and kings because of me, as a testimony to them and the Gentiles.

Mt 10:16-18

Interpretation: You, of gentle hearts, will be exposed to those with hardened hearts and scheming minds. Be alert for those who would judge you and mistreat you. Keep your innocence, but be shrewd as well. Let your heart motivate you and your mind guide you.

Reveal the Truth

So have no fear of them; for nothing is covered up that will not be uncovered, and nothing secret that will not become known. What I say to you in the dark, tell in the light; and what you hear whispered, proclaim from the housetops.

Mt 10:26-27

Interpretation: Fear not, for through you the truth will see the light of day. Teach in public what you learn in private; reveal what has been veiled; and call attention to what has been ignored. Be the voice of God in the world.

Welcome

Whoever welcomes you welcomes me, and whoever welcomes me welcomes the one who sent me. Whoever welcomes a prophet in the name of a prophet will receive a prophet's reward; and whoever welcomes a righteous person in the name of a righteous person will receive the reward of the righteous; and whoever gives a cup of cold water to one of these little ones in the name of a disciple – truly I tell you, none of these will lose their reward.

Mt 10:40-42

Interpretation: Those who receive you with kindness and hospitality also receive me who sent you, and God who sent me. Whether they welcome you because of your prophecy or your righteousness, or only because of your discipleship, they will benefit from your presence.

Acknowledge

Everyone therefore who acknowledges me before others, I also will acknowledge before my Father in heaven; but whoever denies me before others, I also will deny before my Father in heaven.

Mt. 10:32-33

Interpretation: To acknowledge your teacher publicly is to acknowledge the source of your teachings, and the source of your teacher's teachings. Be not ashamed to reveal the Source of your convictions.

Arrive in Peace, Leave in Peace

Whatever town or village you enter, find out who in it is worthy, and stay there until you leave. As you enter the house greet it. If the house is worthy, let your peace come upon it; but if it is not worthy, let your peace return to you. If anyone will not welcome you or listen to your words, shake off the dust from your feet as you leave that house or town. Truly I tell you, it will be more tolerable for the land of Sodom and Gomorrah on the day of judgment than for that town.

Mt 10:11-15

Interpretation: Wherever you go, you will find those who are open to the message you carry and those who are not. Offer the peace of God to all whom you encounter. Stay where you are welcome; leave the place where you are not; but keep your peace about you as you go. Do not allow their disbelief to discourage you in any way. Carry on with faith and purpose; there are those who wait for you.

Serve Without Recompense

You received without payment; give without payment. Take no gold, or silver, or copper in your belts, no bag for your journey, or two tunics, or sandals, or a staff; for laborers deserve their food.

Mt 10:8-10

Interpretation: Gifts from the heart cannot be compensated. What love prompts you to give cannot be repaid. Receive the realm of heaven and pass it on to those who want it. Leave behind the extraneous, take with you only the essential. Trust in the providence of God and the kindness of strangers to provide you with what you need.

Truth

Do not give what is holy to dogs; and do not throw your pearls before swine, or they will trample them underfoot and turn and maul you.

Mt 7:6

Interpretation: To offer sacred truths to those who will not listen is futile and may actually do you harm. Choose your listeners wisely and measure your words appropriately; sow your seeds in tilled and fertile soil.

Go Where You Are Needed

Go nowhere among the Gentiles, and enter no town of the Samaritans, but go rather to the lost sheep of the house of Israel. As you go, proclaim the good news, "The kingdom of heaven has come near."

Mt 10:5-7

Interpretation: Reach out, not to those who will not listen, but to those who may be confused, wounded, or lost, yet are open to believe. Let them know that the realm of heaven is within them ready to be tapped.

The Greatest Among You

You know that the rulers of the Gentiles lord it over them, and their great ones are tyrants over them. It will not be so among you; but whoever wishes to be great among you must be your servant, and whoever wishes to be first among you must be your slave; just as the Son of Man came not to be served but to serve, and to give his life a ransom for many.

Mt 20:25-28

Interpretation: True greatness does not come with authority and power over others, rather, with humility and service to them. If you would be great, serve others. I came into the world to serve and to advocate on behalf of others. You were born to do the same.

A Desert Place

Come away to a deserted place all by yourselves and rest a while.
Mk 6:31

Interpretation: Take the time to leave the crowd and go off by yourselves to rest in solitude and silence. The rigors of life necessitate that you retreat, if only for a little while. Practice the humility of repose so that you may practice the generosity of service.

Endurance

Brother will betray brother to death, and a father his child, and children will rise against parents and have them put to death; and you will be hated by all because of my name. But the one who endures to the end will be saved. When they persecute you in one town, flee to the next; for truly I tell you, you will not have gone through all the towns of Israel before the Son of Man comes.
Mt 10:21-23

Interpretation: There will be great division in the land, even among members of the same family. You who follow my teachings will be outcasts, but your enduring faith will see you through. If one place rejects you, move on to the next. Trust that I am with you wherever you may go.

Family against Family

Do not think that I have come to bring peace to the earth; I have not come to bring peace, but a sword.

For I have come to set a man against his father, and a daughter against her mother, and a daughter-in-law against her mother-in-law; and one's foes will be members of one's own household.

Mt 10:34-36

Interpretation: Ultimately, what I teach brings peace of soul, but not before it brings discord within yourself and among the human family. Before you allow the formation of new perspectives, there must first be the dissolution of the old, and the chaos of transition. Before there can be the union of your mind and spirit, there must first be the tension of opposites and the disunion of reason and faith; and before there can be new life, there must first be the death of habits, traditions, and loyalties.

Trust the Spirit

When they hand you over, do not worry about how you are to speak or what you are to say; for what you are to say will be given to you at that time; for it is not you who speak, but the Spirit of your Father speaking through you.

Mt 10:19-20

Interpretation: When you are called to answer for your beliefs trust that the spirit of God will speak for you and through you. Put your faith not in your clever mind, but in your faithful heart. You will not be muted, but endowed with the word of God.

Before the Loss

The wedding guests cannot mourn as long as the bridegroom is with them, can they? The days will come when the bridegroom is taken away from them, and then they will fast.

Mt 9:15

Interpretation: There will be time enough to grieve what has been lost. For now let us rejoice in one another's presence. The moments before us are precious and irreplaceable. They are all we have.

War

Put your sword back in its place; for all who take the sword will perish by the sword.

Mt 26:52

Interpretation: Abandon your warring ways. Those who make war are destroyed by war. Enter into the realm of heaven through prayer and meditation and discover there a peace you have never known before.

Stay Awake

I am deeply grieved, even to death; remain here, and stay awake with me. Stay awake and pray that you may not come into the time of trial; the spirit indeed is willing, but the flesh is weak.

Mt 26:38, 41

Interpretation: Stand vigil with me in this, our darkest hour. Wake up and pray for the faith to face your moment of truth. The power of your will is insufficient to overcome your natural instinct to survive. Pray for strength of spirit.

Dying to Self

For those who want to save their life will lose it, and those who lose their life for my sake will find it. For what will it profit them if they gain the whole world but forfeit their life? Or what will they give in return for their life.

Mt. 16:25-26

Interpretation: Lay down your life that you may take it up again. Die that you may live. Surrender to the transformational forces of life. Drop your pretentious postures and acknowledge the reality of God's incarnation in you. Put away your illusion of separation and embrace your oneness with all that is.

The Way of the Cross

If any want to become my followers, let them deny themselves and take up their cross daily and follow me.

Lk 9:23

Interpretation: The way of the cross is the way of love. You enter into the place of darkness, the abyss of despair, there to be at one with the forsaken, the miserable, and the crucified. You go there to bring light and compassion in the name of God. At the confluence of the cross your opposites are reconciled, your shattered forces are gathered, and your union with God is consummated.

Made in the USA
Charleston, SC
29 May 2014